D0906575

Caedmon's Song

To the Revs. Clare Dowding, Shari Bledsoe, and Christina van Liew,
St. Hilda's heirs in spirit

– R. A.

To my sister Margaret, who searches for her own song within

– B. S.

Text © 2006 Ruth Ashby
Illustrations © 2006 Bill Slavin
Published in 2006 by Eerdmans Books for Young Readers
An imprint of Wm. B. Eerdmans Publishing Company
255 Jefferson S.E., Grand Rapids, Michigan 49503
P.O. Box 163, Cambridge CB3 9PU U.K.
All rights reserved
Manufactured in China
www.eerdmans.com/youngreaders

06 07 08 09 10 11   8 7 6 5 4 3 2 1

Library of Congress Cataloging-in-Publication Data

Ashby, Ruth.
Caedmon's song / written by Ruth Ashby ; illustrated by Bill Slavin.
p. cm.

ISBN 0-8028-5241-6 (alk. paper)

1. Caedmon – Juvenile literature. 2. Poets, English – Old English, ca. 450-1100 –
Biography – Juvenile literature. I. Slavin, Bill. II. Title.
PR1623.A84 2006
829'.2--dc22
2004010305

The text type is set in Catull.
The illustrations were created with acrylics on gessoed paper.
Gayle Brown, Art Director
Matthew Van Zomeren, Graphic Designer

Caedmon's Song

Written by Ruth Ashby
Illustrated by Bill Slavin

Eerdmans Books for Young Readers

Grand Rapids, Michigan • Cambridge, U.K.

any years ago in the north of England, there lived a cowherd named Caedmon. He dwelled on the grounds of a big abbey, where monks and nuns worked and studied together. But Caedmon was not a monk. His job was to take care of cows: brown cows, brindled cows, cows with long soft eyelashes and short sharp horns. When calves were born, Caedmon found them the warmest corner of the stable to rest in. He slept with cows, and he ate with cows. Cows were his life.

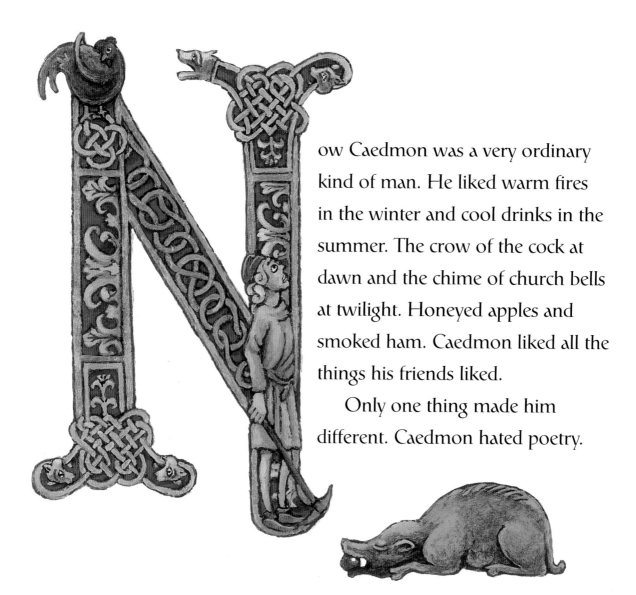

ow Caedmon was a very ordinary kind of man. He liked warm fires in the winter and cool drinks in the summer. The crow of the cock at dawn and the chime of church bells at twilight. Honeyed apples and smoked ham. Caedmon liked all the things his friends liked.

Only one thing made him different. Caedmon hated poetry.

In those days, hardly anyone knew how to read or write. Caedmon couldn't read, and neither could Wilfred the Baker, or Eadfrith the Cooper, or Eadweaner the Swineherd. Frod the Reeve scratched little x's in the dirt to count his sheep. Only the monks in the big abbey where Caedmon worked had books. They copied down the gospels in beautiful flowing script and decorated the pages with golden serpents.

Instead of reading, people recited stories by heart. They sat around the hearth at night, telling of heroes and monsters, great battles fought and fortunes made and lost. On feast days, they passed the harp around the great oak tables so that everyone could sing a poem.

But when the harp reached Caedmon, his thoughts dried up. The words died on his tongue. He opened his mouth and nothing – nothing – came out. It was so embarrassing. No wonder he hated poetry.

ne frosty Saint Stephen's Eve, a feast was held in the great hall of the abbey. While outside the wind blew and snow drifted above the gables, inside guests feasted upon roast mutton and wild boar. Hot spiced ale flowed freely, poured from great goblets of wood and silver.

Caedmon sat close to the fire, warming his frozen feet. His stomach was full, but his mind was troubled. He knew that the moment he dreaded would soon arrive. The storytelling was about to begin.

Thrum! The first note of the harp rang high and clear throughout the hall. "I sing of mighty days gone by," began Wrecca the Minstrel. "Of Scyld, greatest of kings, most worthy of fame."

A hush fell upon the room. Up and down the enormous oak table, revelers sighed in anticipation. Dogs crawled under the benches to chew their bones. Eosric the hawk flew down from the rafters to perch on his master's arm. From the great fire, smoke curled lazily up to the sky — and people dreamed.

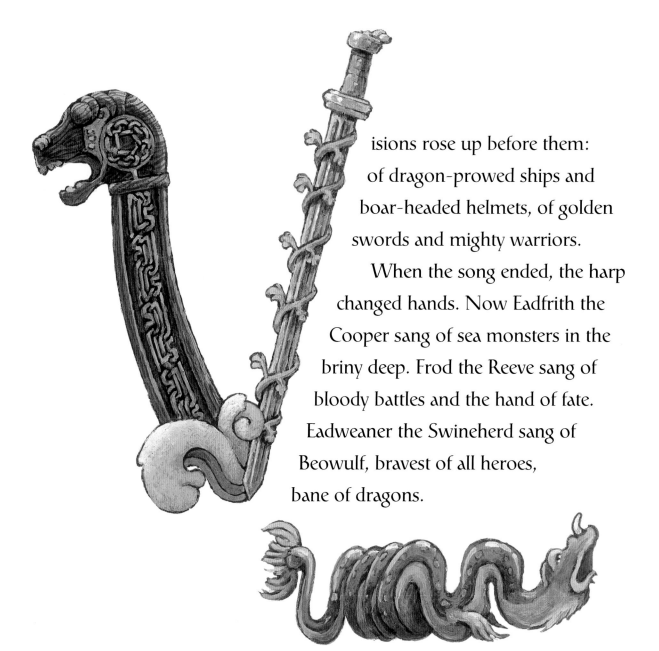

isions rose up before them:
of dragon-prowed ships and
boar-headed helmets, of golden
swords and mighty warriors.

When the song ended, the harp
changed hands. Now Eadfrith the
Cooper sang of sea monsters in the
briny deep. Frod the Reeve sang of
bloody battles and the hand of fate.
Eadweaner the Swineherd sang of
Beowulf, bravest of all heroes,
bane of dragons.

Finally it was Caedmon's turn. The harp was his.

"Caedmon, give us a tale!" shouted Wilfred the Baker. Others raised their drinking horns in the air. "By Saint Stephen, we want a song!" they cried.

Caedmon stood up and gazed around the hall. This time he would do it. He too would sing a song of great warriors and fearsome battles.

A thousand images flashed through his mind. Thrum! He plucked loudly at the harp. "A great many years ago . . ."

His voice faltered. The harp fell silent.

"Long ago and far away . . ." he began again.

It was no use. The words would not come. Caedmon thrust the harp at the next man and wrapped his cloak around him. Furious and ashamed, he stomped down the hall and pushed open the great ash doors.

He had failed again.

Caedmon stormed out into the darkness. The blizzard
had ceased, and mounds of snow had drifted across the
moors. He shivered, as cold and bitter as the night.

Then a cloud floated across the sky. The full moon burst
forth, and the world was transformed. Hills, valleys,
mountains, and seas sparkled with a million pinpoints
of light. Caedmon looked up at the stars glittering above
him. His anger and shame melted away. It is all
so calm and beautiful, he thought. As beautiful
as the first day of creation.

He trudged back to the cowshed. Inside, the air was warm with the breath of cows. Caedmon made sure his animals were comfortable for the night. Then he crawled onto his sleeping mat and fell asleep.

Caedmon dreamed, and in his dream a young man came into the cowshed and sat down. "Caedmon," the man called out.

Caedmon opened his eyes.

"Caedmon, why are you sleeping?" the man asked. "Tonight is the Feast of Saint Stephen. It is time for celebration."

"I left the feast early," Caedmon replied.

"Ah, you left because you did not want to sing," the man said.

Who was this man who seemed to know so much about him? "No, I left because I could not sing," Caedmon corrected him. "There is no poetry in me."

"There is poetry in everyone," the man replied. "Now, sing me a song."

"But I have nothing to sing about."

"Surely you do. Sing about the things you know."

What did he know?

Caedmon thought.

As his dream continued, Caedmon thought about the warm breath of cows on a frosty morning and the bleats of newborn calves. He thought about cool green dawns and fiery red sunsets. About meadows sparkling with dew and hawks circling the sky. About gray seas and purple flowers. He thought about the stars.

And he opened his mouth and sang:

Praise we now the Keeper of heaven's kingdom,
The mind of the mighty Maker,
The Glorious Father who made
The world and all its wonders;

How first he created the roof of heaven
For us, the children of men;
Then the holy Creator, the eternal Lord,
Gave the earth to people,
This middle earth to be our home.

he next morning when Caedmon
awoke, he remembered his dream.
Filled with joy and wonder, he
sought out Frod the Reeve and told
his friend what had happened.

He recited his song. Frod was
astounded. "Surely this is a miracle!"
Frod exclaimed. "We must tell the
abbess. She will know what
to do."

Abbess Hilda was in the library reading a prayer book. When she listened to Caedmon's story and heard his song, she rejoiced.

"We must give thanks," she told the cowherd, "for you have received a gift from God."

And she asked Caedmon to give up his life as a cowherd and become a monk, for the abbey needed such an inspired creator of songs.

From that day forward, Caedmon was a poet. He moved into the monastery with all the other monks and told them stories. Caedmon sang of the creation of the world and the beginnings of the human race. He sang of Noah and the flood and of Moses and the Promised Land. He sang of David, and he sang of Jesus.

Soon Caedmon was known throughout the land. Children everywhere memorized his special song, his first hymn of praise. And on feast days, when people gathered around great oak tables, they no longer sang about bloody battles and dreadful monsters. They sang Caedmon's songs and poems instead.

Caedmon lived until his death in great comfort and happiness, and he visited his cows every day.

Biographical Note

Caedmon was a real person, and the story of his song, called "Caedmon's Hymn," may well be true. The tale comes to us from Bede, England's earliest historian. According to Bede, Caedmon worked as a cowherd at the monastery of Whitby in Yorkshire in about 660 A.D. He hated reciting poetry in public, and one evening, when the storytelling began, Caedmon left the feast and went out to the cowshed. There he dreamed of a man who called him by name and told him to sing. Caedmon replied that he could not sing. But when the man asked that he sing of the beginning of creation, Caedmon opened his mouth, and the words came.

Though Caedmon went on to compose many religious songs, most of them were lost. Only one poem is known to us today. "Caedmon's Hymn" is the earliest known poem to be written down in the English language. For this reason, Caedmon is called the first English poet.

You wouldn't be able to understand the English that Caedmon spoke. His English was actually "Old English," and it included many words we no longer use. However, many of our most commonly used words are still recognizable in Old English. For instance, in Old English, "I" was "ic," "he" was "he," "life" was "lif," and "man" was "mann." But many words are completely different.

Here is what "Caedmon's Hymn" looked like in Old English:

Nu sculon herigean   heofonrices Weard
Meotodes meahte   and his modgeþanc
weorc Wuldorfæder,   swa he wundra gehwæs
ece Drihten   or onstealde
He ærest sceop   ielda bearnum
heofan to hrofe,   halig Scyppend;
Ða middangeard   moncynnes Weard,
ece Drihten,   æfter teode
firum foldan,   Frea ælmihtig.